The Art of the 'Ask'
Get in the Fundraising Groove

Connie S. Pheiff

The Art of the Ask: Get into the Fundraising Groove
Copyright © 2013 by Connie S. Pheiff. All Rights Reserved
www.conniepheiffspeaks.com

ISBN: 978-0-9893202-0-7
Published by Dragonfly Press
Printed in the United States of America
2013

For information about custom editions, special sales, premium and corporate purchases, please contact Dragonfly Press Sales Department at 570.341.2002 or info@conniepheiffspeaks.com.

Dedication

To my former employers…
You gave me the entrepreneurial spirit to share my wisdom and
courage through my speaking, coaching, and writing.

Author's Note

I wrote this book to help nonprofit staff and experienced fundraising professionals excel in today's tough fundraising environment. The nonprofit sector continues to be ravaged by changes—everything from scandals to the realignment of borders of national organizations. No matter what level you are in the organization, the information in this book will help you understand that Attitude + Passion = Results (A+P=R), and determine if you have the right attitude to be working in the nonprofit sector.

The *Art of the Ask* is actually quite simple:

- You make your ask.
- You make your case.
- You show the benefits.
- Then you stop talking.

The teachings and stories in this book can be read from different perspectives: current executive directors, aspiring executive directors, development officers, board members, and community stakeholders.

Whether the organization you work for is large or small, this book gives you the tools to determine if you are in the right place in your career. "Large" is the equivalent of state and national NPOs. "Small" is the equivalent of an organization that does not carry a charter from big brother. In the end, all NPOs need to have a local presence with grassroots efforts. Donors need to know, like, and respect you. Unfortunately, organizations are looking at the economies of scale and closing local offices. This, in my opinion, negatively affects the organization's fundraising efforts.

Philanthropy giving is not disappearing. Giving simply looks different these days, and we need to be open to the ways of work. With change come new opportunities. The big change we're realizing is that the world is much more flat and connected than we ever thought possible. This means you have greater opportunities to increase your fundraising efforts.

Are you in the right position? You may have a passion for your organization's mission and cause, but do you have what it takes to "ask" for the dollars? My coach has taught me that 85 percent of success is having the confidence from looking within. It's time for you to take that look within for yourself.

Contents

Foreword   11

Introduction   15

Chapter 1
What is Fundraising?   19

Chapter 2
You are Your Organization's Most Precious Resource   21

Chapter 3
Develop the Proper Attitude   29

Chapter 4
Know What You Want   33

Chapter 5
Get a Coach   37

Chapter 6
Spread the Word   41

Chapter 7
Get Donors to Call You   45

Chapter 8
What to Say to Donors … and What Not to Say   49

Chapter 9
Go for "The Ask"   53

Chapter 10
Overcome Rejection   57

Chapter 11
Stay the Course   61

Chapter 12
When Donors Leave   63

Chapter 13
Manage Your Time ...Or It Will Manage You   67

Chapter 14
The 4 Biggest Mistakes a Fundraiser Makes   71

Chapter 15
Make Yourself Stand Out   75

Chapter 16
Creating Donor Loyalty   81

Chapter 17
Finding New Donors   85

Chapter 18
Asses Yourself   91

Recommended Reading & Resources   97

About the Author   99

"Remember the words of the Lord Jesus,
how he said, it is more blessed to give
than to receive."
~Acts 20:35

"We make a living by what we
get, but we make a life by what
we give."
~Winston Churchill

*"In the long run, we shape our lives, and we shape
ourselves. The process never ends
until we die. And the choices we make are
ultimately our own responsibility".*
~Eleanor Roosevelt

"Ignite your Passion."
~Connie S. Pheiff

Foreword

We've seen Jeff Skoll (eBay), Mark Zuckerberg (Facebook), Bill Gates (Microsoft), Warren Buffet (Berkshire Hathaway), Michael Bloomberg (New York City Mayor and founder of Bloomberg Financial News Service), and others commit to The Giving Pledge—pledging to give away at least half of their wealth to philanthropic causes. These individuals built for-profit businesses but then structured those profits to be plowed into worthy endeavors.

The key concept in understanding how to tap into these rich resources is not to simply raise your hand as a nonprofit organization. These wealthy donors are looking far beyond just the legal structure to the very things that allowed their businesses to be so successful. In the for-profit world, things like poor financial controls, inability to adapt, fierce competition, ineffective management, and technology and social media changes cause businesses to close or to be swallowed by similar organizations. Knowledgeable business leaders are quick to recognize similar challenges in nonprofit companies.

Innovative types of organizations are blurring the distinctions between for-profit and nonprofit entities. New terms like social entrepreneurship, ethical capitalism, and "B" corporations are emerging and showing their ability to address issues like pollution, poverty, and illiteracy that were historically only the domain of the nonprofit world. John Sage (Pura Vida Coffee), Tom Szaky (TerraCycle), Blake Mycoskie (TOMS Shoes), and many others are leading the way with for-profit businesses that are doing well while doing good. In today's economic workplace you can change the world, address poverty or pollution, make the world a better place ... *and make money* in the process.

Bottom line: The legal structure of an organization is less important than having a worthy mission to fulfill, as well as a business structure that is efficient and compelling. Wealthy donors expect business excellence in the causes they choose to support.

As clarified in *The Art of the Ask*, "Fundraising is a business; it's not your mother's charity anymore." And the people in that business are the face and voice of it. Ultimately donors give to people they know, like, and trust. You are selling an idea, a cause, a better way of life, or a solution to a recognized problem. In the world of selling we often tell people that true, professional selling is simply sharing enthusiasm. And fortunately, that enthusiasm can be enhanced by proper attitude and confidence, coupled with knowing when to be silent.

To compete in today's marketplace we have to compete on quality and value to earn the right to ask people to support our causes. We can't offer shoddy service, inefficient money management, substandard necklaces, or second-rate coffee and expect people to get excited about helping us in our worthy endeavors. We have to believe we are the very best. We have to be proud of what we are representing and then hold our heads high as we invite people to be part of something great. Our passion for what we are doing can then exceed any fear or sense of inadequacy.

You are reading a tool that will enhance your ability to do something great. *The Art of the Ask* provides the steps to standing above the crowd. The organization you represent deserves more than just adequate resources. You can tap into the rich resources of wealth waiting to be released into your care.

Being excellent at raising resources requires more than being part of a worthy organization. *The Art of the Ask* can put you in the top 5 percent of fundraising experts. This success, as in any area of life, is not luck. Rather, it's when preparation meets opportunity. Enjoy your *preparation*.

~Dan Miller, coach and author of
48 Days to the Work You Love

Introduction

You can do a simple Internet search and find many quotes about giving—many quotes that tell you the only thing that really matters is your attitude. After years of fundraising (too many to mention), I know this belief is true. *Your attitude is everything when it comes to fundraising.*

My fundraising initiatives began with the small PTA bake sales. Over time my passion for fundraising expanded, and eventually I was asking for big dollars for the Chamber of Commerce of the United States.

As a fundraiser and former employee of the nonprofit sector, I know how valuable your time can be. So let me get right to the point: **This book is a how-to for those who face fundraising with fear. It will show you how Attitude + Passion = Results (A+P=R)**

First, realize that if you fear fundraising then you are in the wrong position. When coaching executive directors, development officers, and board members, I find that most have a passion for the organization they represent. I also find that most have a fear of fundraising. In this book we will address why having the right people in the fundraising role, as well as having the right attitude, will make your fundraising efforts so much more productive.

I will not talk about the historical philosophies that surround fundraising. If you are like me, you have already listened to CDs, read fundraising books, and attended gobs of seminars to learn how to fundraise. In plain language I will provide examples of real world experience and what I recommend as the most valuable pieces of information you need to be a successful fundraiser.

My best fundraising efforts were with the Chamber of Commerce of the United States. My work was directly with the President of the Chamber and Senior Vice Presidents. Initially, I started as a telephone sales representative. (Hey, we all have to start somewhere, right?) I was quickly promoted to downtown Washington D.C., right across from the White House. I made it! I was working in the District! Honestly, this was one of the best times of my working career.

My position was to work with the executive team to develop a 16-month plan to revitalize the Chamber of Commerce of the United States. Here are the highlights.

I.   Fix the infrastructure through finances and membership recruitment, and put retention systems in place.
II.   Reorganize the membership system.
III. Enhance the commercial operations and partnerships.
IV.   Strengthen relationships of state and local Chambers of Commerce, government officials, and the media.
V.   Advance the core agenda.
VI.   Defend businesses against attacks on the enterprise system.

Funding, in large amounts, needed to happen for these changes to take place. For nearly 18 months, a 40-city tour took place where we visited corridors of power in Washington, D.C. and across the country asking for BIG money.

Of course, that's just one example of my success. In this book I will share best practices in the industry—the ones I learned from my mentors as well as the ones I gleamed from the school of hard knocks. You'll learn how your attitude is the key to fundraising success (and how to change yours if you need to), as well as hands-on strategies that will make your fundraising efforts more prosperous.

Remember, a nonprofit is a business; it's not your mother's charity anymore. This book is not meant to simplify your existence, but to streamline your efforts. Refer to these pages time and time again, and you'll soon become the next fundraising superstar.

Chapter 1
What is Fundraising?

According to Webster's Dictionary, fundraising or fund rais-ing (also development) is the process of soliciting and gathering voluntary contributions of money or other resources, by requesting donations from individuals, businesses, charitable foundations, or governmental agencies. Although fundraising typically refers to efforts to gather money for nonprofit organi-zations, it is sometimes used to refer to the identification and solicitation of investors or other sources of capital for for-profit enterprises.

Traditionally, fundraising consisted mostly of asking for dona-tions on the street or at people's doors, such as selling Girl Scout cookies. These days, fundraising takes on many forms as social networking is emerging; however, grassroots fundraising continues to be the best method for increasing funds. From a direct "ask" for money to events and program sales, fundraising is a constant for a nonprofit organization.

Why is Fundraising Important?

Although an organization is called a "nonprofit," fundraising needs to include the cost of doing business. Today, a nonprofit is not your mother's charity; most are well-run machines.

The definition of a nonprofit is "not to profit." But if there was no profit, then how could the organization turn the lights on in the morning, pay staff salaries, conduct staff training, or hire a professional fundraiser? The cost of running a nonprofit can be enormous. Today, donors are keener on an organization's mission, and when making a donation they will designate the funds to go directly to a specific program. But again, the organization needs funds just to function, much less provide whatever program or service they offer.

For your nonprofit to be successful—and for you to be a successful fundraiser—you need to adopt a new two-word descriptor for what fundraising is all about. Those two words are:

1. Consistency – If you want your funders to return year after year, you and your organization must display consistency in your message and your tactics.
2. Attitude – Whether you're asking for a large amount or a small one, whether from an individual or a company, your confident attitude plays a huge role in how the donor responds.

Before we delve into the core information, please note that I don't know of any magic wand or secret formula. Fundraising is hard work. To be successful at it requires a consistent, persistent, determined, and intentional attitude when making "the ask." Now it's time to discover how to be that person.

Chapter 2
You are Your Organization's
Most Precious Resource

For any nonprofit, people are the organization's most precious resource. When the wrong people are taking on the fundraising role, the results can be damaging to the organization. Having your best and brightest do "the ask" is great, but you also need an individual with the right attitude and passion. Then everyone wins.

Now, let's face reality. An organization with successful campaigns can say they have a robust staff, each person with independent responsibilities and a focus on an area of expertise. But we know that the nonprofit sector is not always so fortunate. All too often, nonprofits must rely on committed volunteers and board members to work on the fundraising initiatives. Add in the Pareto Principle (or the 80/20 rule) where you have 20% of the people doing 80% of the work, and you can see how difficult it can be for organizations (and individual fundraisers) to thrive.

In fact, in many nonprofits, it's common for a staff member to wear the hat of multiple positions. For example, I was once hired as the executive director for a local United Way. My background is that of fundraising and leadership. Before long I learned the board had a different plan for me: they also wanted me to be the bookkeeper. I quickly expressed my concerns, because bookkeeping is not one of my strengths. But because of funding, the board could not hire a bookkeeper, so it became me. And I admit it...bookkeeping is not something I enjoy or look forward to doing every day. So I strongly recommend that if you are wearing multiple hats, be sure all those hats consist of a job you know and are capable of doing. Otherwise you will go bonkers!

Know Your Team

Fundraising efforts have multiple individuals involved, including:

> ➢ The executive director (CEO). In addition to oversight of the mission and programs, the executive director has the responsibility of being the "face of the community." If the executive director is not seen or known in the community, then he or she should be replaced immediately.

> ➢ Development officer. According to *The Nonprofit Times* (2011), the mean salary of a good development officer commands $65,000. Unless you are an organization that has the financial ability to hire at this level, the executive director, a part-time development officer, or a volunteer will be leading the fundraising initiative. A good development officer will have good writing and verbal communication skills.

> ➢ All staff members. The person leading the fundraising needs to keep the staff up-to-date on the initiatives. Why? Because *everyone in the organization is responsible for fundraising*. Without fundraising, there are no

funds for payroll and no staff to deliver programs. This is a joint effort, period!

➢ Committed volunteers. You will be able to find volunteers who are committed to the mission of the organization. For example, my mother teaches sewing and design. She is also a cancer survivor. Each year since her recovery she holds a fashion show with her students. The proceeds of the show go directly to the American Cancer Society. Do you think the students' families are willing to pay to see their loved ones in a fashion show? Of course! Do you think the American Cancer Society praises Mom for her hard work of putting together the fundraising program without asking for help? Most definitely! Mom has a passion for the mission of the American Cancer Society. You can find people just like Mom in your community.

When you find volunteers, keep them fired up so they build excitement for the organization, which encourages others to join. When I was working with a local Chamber of Commerce office, I started with 6 volunteer ambassadors and grew the group to 86 people. We worked hard together—and played hard together. That excitement, energy, and camaraderie attracted similar people to get involved.

➢ Membership. Not all nonprofit organizations have membership. You may! The Girl Scouts are a membership organization. My work with the Girl Scouts involved the Green Hat Society. This is a group of adult Girl Scouts who are still dedicated to the mission. The development of this group led to endowments.

➢ Board of Directors. Most, I repeat, most board members join because they believe in your mission. It needs to be strongly stated in the board agreement that the number one responsibility of a board member is to give, get, or get off. (Many organizations forget this little detail!) Of course, I have seen organizations go overboard by stating an amount a board member must give annually … or get off. I was on one of those boards, and before they could tell me to get off, I resigned! The lesson: Never tell someone how much to give. What if they want to give more?

Be sure you are recognizing your board for their work. Board members are volunteers who often have full-time jobs, family, and other outside interests. Board members and committed volunteers are there to support the organization; you need to support them. Recognition goes a long way. Remember, honey is sweeter than vinegar!

➢ Outside coach (if you are able to pay, I recommend). If you select to hire a coach, it is important the paid staff understand how to surrender control. Yes, this has been an issue. A coach can help you design the fundraising plan, address board concerns, lead board retreats and training of the plan, and create grassroots efforts where the organization and board can work together toward a successful goal. Coaching will develop the executive director into a successful engine for the organization. You can find a coach that will write grants, develop the marketing plan, and handle direct mailings, individual solicitations, and board retreats. For more ideas go to www.idealist.org.

When you hire an outside coach, be aware of the legal matters that surround this type of worker. This is not an employee, and if you treat the person as one you will find yourself in legal trouble.

Get Your Board Involved

I can't express enough the importance of board participation. Each board member should be a cheerleader in your corner who lets the community know your nonprofit is the go-to organization for philanthropy giving.

There is no limit to your board's participation and fundraising efforts. However, keep in mind that these are volunteers and they may have different interests or time constraints. Right from the get-go, make sure your board members are on board (pun intended!). Ask them to help with planning and executing the fundraising plan.

For example, perhaps your board members enjoy a good party. If so, ask them to plan a special event, host a house party, or initiate a giving program in their workplace. Other ways the board can be involved include representing the organization in the community, providing names of philanthropists, "asking" for dollars, doing personal letter writing, and personally thanking the donors for their financial and volunteer contributions.

If you have ever been on a board, then you know the constant cry for help board members hear from fundraisers. Now that you are on the other side of the table you need to be cognizant of when enough is enough. This is one of the reasons why board members should have term limitations. I worked with organizations with no limitations, and it was chaos! Board limitations need to be addressed and clearly labeled in the by-laws.

Too often, individuals join a board and have no idea how to best contribute to the cause. Help your board members determine their strengths. The person could be so committed that he or she will do whatever it takes to move the organization forward. But he or she needs your help to determine what that something could be. You live this work day in and day out while the volunteer helps a day or two per month. When your board members see where they fit, they will be more engaged and motivated.

Grant Din, the executive director of Asian Neighborhood Design (www.andnet.org) in San Francisco, has created a great board set up. As he explained, "We have one board member who's a development director at another nonprofit, which is perfect, because he can emphasize the importance of fundraising and not have others tune him out the way they might if a paid staff member said the same thing. We also have another board member who has really pushed for full participation by the board, and the two of them have created more of a giving and getting environment."

Your board members need to feel wanted and appreciated for their hard work. Happy board members mean results!

Also, be sure your board members understand the mission of the organization. Just because an individual becomes a board member, do not assume they know all there is to know about your organization.

When new board members join, take some time for show and tell. This does not mean you have an orientation for each new board member. Instead, select a time of year, typically at the beginning of the fiscal calendar, where you induct new board members. Following the induction, ask a seasoned board member to lead a program to educate the new members and allow time for questions and answers. You can create colorful pie charts to explain the financials, and a PowerPoint presentation to explain the program's mission and work of the organization. Let them know the significance of the organization and all the hard work you do for the community. When board members feel your passion, they will exude that passion to the community ... and dollars will follow.

Volunteers are Priceless!

Who are your volunteers and where do they come from? Your volunteers will come from all walks of life. Corporations often have programs where employees are encouraged to volunteer in the community. Students need to give X number of community hours for class credit if they are looking to be submitted into college or the National Honor Society. Retirees want to contribute to society and continue to be a huge pool of potential volunteers. Criminals re-entering society need to do community service. You can research organizations in your community that work with these programs, such as The Salvation Army and The MacAuley Center.

Also, contact local organizations, including high schools and colleges with leadership programs, to let them know you have volunteer opportunities available. If you have the financial resources you can contact the Area on Aging and hire a part-time senior aide. You will put a smile on a person's face when you give them a sense of purpose.

Just as we discussed board training, we also need to address volunteer training and getting a commitment. When you develop a formal process for volunteer training and explain the mission and programs of the organization, you will make the volunteers' experience more comfortable—for you and the volunteers. Know each volunteer's strengths and use his or her talents accordingly. If they are willing to work in the fundraising office and do not like to make "the ask," you can have them write thank-you notes or enter data into the donation software system (be sure to set parameters of how to enter the information; otherwise you could end up with duplications).

Volunteers need to be treated the same as staff members. When a volunteer is working on your time, policies and procedures must be followed. I had to fire volunteers on several occasions.

One of the firings caused such a mess with the organization that we had to get an attorney involved. The volunteer just refused to leave. Your volunteers are the face of the organization. If you have a volunteer bad mouthing the organization or you, get to the bottom of the issue right away. If you don't deal with the issue head-on, it will only fester and get worse.

Of course, have fun with your volunteers. But remember, you, your staff, and your volunteers are the face of the organization. I would suggest no pole dancing on weekends.

Chapter 3
Develop the Proper Attitude

People give to people they know, like, and trust. And people give to people, not to causes. Your ability to make "the ask" and to create a positive image of the organization in the community is essential. Remember, your success largely depends upon your ability to connect with people and your attitude toward fundraising.

So, what stops most people from being successful at fundraising? A deep-rooted fear of rejection.

In other words, the thing that's getting in your way of success is YOU.

Fear of rejection is human nature. But did you know that you have a choice in how you handle rejection? It's true. You can choose to allow rejection to pull you down or you can choose to allow rejection to pick you up.

It's all about the attitude you choose to embrace.

How do I achieve and maintain a positive attitude when fundraising, despite any rejection I may face?

Attitude is a state of mind. Whether your attitude is positive or negative is a choice. No matter what's happening around you, no matter what kind of rejection you're facing, you're in control of your attitude and you determine what your attitude is.

We all have a negative sense and a positive sense that can shape our attitude. A negative sense is based in fear. It's about procrastination, self-doubt, uncertainty, and doom. It's what makes people say things like, "I'm so unlucky" or "I never catch a break" or "The sky is falling." Do you know anyone like this?

Have you ever gone to a church picnic or school event where there was a raffle? How many times do you hear people say, "I never win anything"? When I go to those events, I always win something. I don't really try; it just happens that way. I think it's because I choose to see the possibilities rather than the obstacles.

If your mental attitude continually says, "I'm unlucky," it's time to turn that around.

A positive sense is based in opportunity. It's about self-confidence, determination, achievement, winning, success, good fortune, and a sense of a sunny day. I've found that you can transform a rainy, miserable day into a sunny day at any time. You just have to choose to do so.

Here's a quick story to illustrate the power of a positive attitude. A few years ago, my position as CEO of the Girl Scouts left me. At about the same time I learned that I was adopted...Dad was not who he said he was. When I received the news I was in shock, disbelief, and without realizing it, I went into depression. Not the clinical version, but I became sick, had nine surgeries in two-years. I soon realized it was my attitude that was causing me to be ill. I turned myself around by shifting my attitude. One step I took was to go back to school. My life goal was to complete my Bachelor's degree. As of this writing it's been six years. Today, I completed my bachelor's degree in business administration. I also earned my Masters in Business Science, and Masters in Public Administration. Yeah me!

If you ask how I overcame this life altercation, I will tell you it was because of a positive attitude. I decided I was going to fight the illness and not let it bring me down. I refused to feel sorry for myself or behave like a sick person. The entire time I was battling my illness I continued going to school and learning as much as I can about people, organizational behavior, and politics — even when I was recovering from my surgeries. Keeping a positive attitude the entire time made all the difference.

What specific strategies can I employ to maintain a positive attitude?

There are a number of things you can do to improve your attitude. Some things I've found that work well for fundraisers are:

- Surround yourself with positive people. If you're continually with people who are negative, you're going to "catch" their attitude.

- Read positive books and listen to positive CDs. At the end of this book I give you my list of recommended books to read (or listen to on CD). A good one to start with is *Three Feet from Gold: Turn Your Obstacles into Opportunities* by Sharon L. Lechter CPA and Greg S. Reid.

- Say things in a positive way. Rather than say, "I can't," say, "How can I?" That means "I can't raise money" turns into "How can I raise money?" From this day forward, the word "can't" is no longer in your dictionary.

- Believe in yourself. You can do whatever you put your mind to. As Henry Ford said, "Whether you think you can or think you can't, you're right."

- Don't listen to other people. Don't listen to the negative ones, the jealous ones, or the uninformed ones. People will always tell you "you're crazy," "no one can do that," and "it's impossible." Don't believe them.

- Pick yourself up. At some point, you're going to fall. You're going to encounter obstacles and road bumps. When you do, remember that it's okay. Just pick yourself right back up into it.

When it comes to attitude, you always have a choice. You can be negative and blame other people for your woes and failures, or you can step out, overcome, and show the world what a great fundraiser can do. The choice is yours. What do you choose?

Chapter 4
Know What You Want

One of the keys to being a superb fundraiser is to know what you want—what you really, really want. That means you need to set S.M.A.R.T. goals.

A goal is nothing more than a dream with a plan and a deadline. Creating that plan and deadline around your dream is all about S.M.A.R.T. goal setting.

S.M.A.R.T. stands for:
- Specific – A specific goal has a much greater chance of being accomplished than a general goal. Goals must be clear and unambiguous; vagaries and platitudes have no place in goal setting.
- Measurable – Establish concrete criteria for measuring progress toward the attainment of each goal you set. When you measure your progress, you stay on track, reach your target dates, and experience the exhilaration of achievement that spurs you on to continued effort required to reach your goal.
- Attainable – Goals must be realistic and attainable. The best goals require you to stretch a bit to achieve them, but they aren't extreme.

- Relevant – To be relevant, a goal must represent an objective toward which you are both willing and able to work. Your goal is probably relevant if you truly believe that it can be accomplished.
- Time-Oriented – If you want to accomplish a goal, when do you want to accomplish it by? "Someday" won't work. But if you anchor it within a timeframe, "by January 1st," then you've set your unconscious mind into motion to begin working on the goal.

With the idea of S.M.A.R.T. goals in mind, ask yourself...
- Where do I want to be a year from today?
- Where do I want the organization to be a year from today?
- How am I going to get there?

Write your answers down! If you don't write them down you're going to forget your answers quickly. In fact, the main reason people don't achieve their goals is because they don't write them down!

After you have your goals written down, do your own personal SWOT analysis. What are your strengths, weaknesses, opportunities, and threats that are going to either help you or get in your way of reaching your goals? Write these down too.

Should I share my goals with others?

Depending on your organization and your goals, you may want to share your goals with others. Perhaps someone can help you achieve the goal in some way (by providing resources, leads, etc.). Or maybe having some outside accountability, like a coach, will keep you motivated to achieve your goals. Of course, if you don't feel comfortable sharing your goals for whatever reason, then don't. Don't put any undue stress on yourself.

My goal seems so big. What's the best way to approach it?

No matter how large or small your goal is, create an action plan to attaining it. Break the goal down into manageable chunks and then state deadlines for completing each segment of the larger goal.

For example, if you make a goal to lose weight, you know you need to exercise and go on a diet. So your first segment of the goal is to create a weekly diet plan. Then, in addition to that weekly plan, the next segment of your goal is to join a gym. Once you have the membership, the next segment of your goal is to actually go to the gym, and so on. So it's about setting smaller goals that enable you to achieve your ultimate goal.

No matter what your goal is, keep it clearly in sight—both literally and figuratively. Post your goals on your office wall so you can look at them every day. Remember, you get what you focus on. What are you going to focus on today?

Chapter 5
Get a Coach

I have had several mentors or coaches in my life. At the time, I didn't think of these people as coaches or mentors, but looking back now, I see that they really were.

No matter where you are in your fundraising career, don't be afraid to seek out a coach[1]. Look for somebody who appears to be a successful fundraiser—a person you admire or would want to emulate. You could also seek out a professional coach—someone you pay a fee for their coaching services. Either way, it'll be an investment in yourself you'll never regret.

What are some guidelines to keep in mind when working with a coach?

- Use your coach wisely. Don't use or abuse your privileges with them. Your coach is going to take pride in your growth.
- Acknowledge your coach and show that you did what they suggested. Did it work or not work?

---

[1] You can get more information about coaching by calling 570.341.2002 or 570.906.4395. Or send an email to connie@conniepheiffspeaks.com.

- Share freely with your coach. Don't hold back. If you want their guidance, they need to know how to best help you.
- Let them help you. You will have days when you're feeling down. Your coach's job is to help pull you back up. When they extend their hand, take it.
- Respect their wisdom. You're asking this person for help because they've "been there and done that." When they give you guidance, take it, no matter how contrary to your thinking it may seem. That's the point of having a coach—to have someone help you see things in different ways.

Throughout my career, coaches have been a major part of my success and growth.

Does the coaching relationship always have to be a formal one?

The coaching may come from a formal coaching relationship or it may come from someone who doesn't even realize they are being a coach to you in some way.

For example, when I worked for the Chamber of Commerce of the United States, my boss was a wonderful coach, although he had no idea of it at the time. One of the best ways to learn is to sit and watch/listen to someone, and that's what I did with him. I would watch him make a fundraising call. Or I would watch him approach a donor in person and I'd listen to what he'd say to them. Then I would mirror what he did, and I found it worked for me. So although he didn't realize it, he was coaching me.

In fact, I learned one of my biggest lessons from watching this guy. Most people in fundraising have heard that when you're asking for the money, the one who speaks first loses. I had never heard that before until I went on a meeting with my boss.

One day while we were visiting a prospective donor, after he asked for the money, my boss just sat there in silence. And he didn't make a sound. I was getting nervous. *Why isn't he saying anything? I thought. Why isn't he closing this?*

Finally, the prospective donor spoke. He said, "Okay. Here's my money."

> *The Art of Asking*
>
> • *You make your ask.*
>
> • *Your make your case.*
>
> • *Your show the benefits.*
>
> • *Then you stop talking.*

Later, when I asked my boss why he sat there in silence, he said, "That's the art of asking. You make your ask, you make your case, you show the benefits, and then you stop talking." It was a lesson I never forgot.

You interact with so many people on a daily basis. Who are you taking advice from? Make sure you're learning from the right people.

Chapter 6
Spread the Word

A good fundraiser tells everyone about the nonprofit and its mission. That means you have to approach donors—both new and established—and consistently give information about your organization. Even if someone has given money every year for the past decade, you need to keep the conversation going so the nonprofit and how it benefits the community stays top of mind.

Most people you'll be contacting have either shown an interest in the organization in the past, or they have given in some way—either money, time, or in kind products/services. Therefore, you're technically dealing with warm contacts rather than cold ones. That alone should ease any fears, increase your confidence, and make your job easier.

What's the best way to get information to donors?

Many people in fundraising think they need a glitzy brochure and other sales materials to present to donors. In reality, your donors don't want to see that because they don't want their donated money being spent that way. If you get the brochure production donated, that's great; just make sure you clearly state that somewhere in the brochure. The same goes for any other media outlets where you may advertise, including billboards, radio and television ads, etc.

Additionally, if you're mailing that brochure or sales material, you have to pay for the postage. That alone can add up to a lot. And again, it's an expense donors don't want their money going toward.

Social media is a low-cost marketing option, but remember that the older generation hasn't embraced it as readily. So if you rely primarily on social media to get your information out there, you're missing out on a large pool of potential donors.

When it comes to spreading your information, the best approach is to have multiple balls in the air. In other words, if you know someone wants to see a brochure, then send them one. If you know someone loves social media, then connect with them there. If you know someone prefers phone calls, then pick up the phone and call them. Do what each donor likes best. I still find the best approach is the old fashioned way—face-to-face.

What's the NPO guru's secret weapon for getting the word out?

The one thing I find works best is to send a personal, handwritten note. In fact, I believe in handwritten notes above anything else. It's that personal touch that makes me stand out to donors.

I also find that picking up the phone and calling someone gets the results I want and expect. As a fundraiser, you simply cannot have call reluctance. And if you're calling warm contacts, why should you fear calling them?

If you're calling a big donor, you'll want to schedule a time to meet with them face-to-face. So you tell them that right up-front: "I want to meet with you. All I need is 10 minutes of your time." Then you meet with them. That's how you get the information to them. It's about having the confidence to pick up the phone, to be direct, and to meet them face-to-face. If you can't do that, then someone else (from another organization) will … and that person will ultimately get your money.

How do I get past the gatekeeper when I call?

If you're calling someone at a corporation, chances are the person you need to reach will have an assistant—a gatekeeper. As you know, this person's job is to carefully screen all calls to make sure only the ones his or her boss really want get through. That's why you want to always be polite and professional to the gatekeeper. Get this person on your side by addressing him or her by name and being friendly.

You can read many sales books on "techniques" for getting past the gatekeeper, but I suggest a simpler approach. Rather than play games or use sales techniques, just be upfront with the gatekeeper. For example, after you request to speak to the person and the gatekeeper asks, "What is this in reference to?" you say, "I'm calling John because he's been a supporter of the Salvation Army for the past seven years. It's our annual campaign time, and I'm calling to see how much he's going to support us again this year."

Yes, it really is as easy as that. Be upfront and be genuine and you'll get your information out there.

Ultimately, the more you know who your donors are, the more comfortable you'll be talking with them. So find out as much as you can about the individual, about their business, and about their passion. Who are you going to call today?

Chapter 7
Get Donors to Call You

New and experienced fundraisers always ask me, "How do I get donors to return my call?" The answer: Be persistent.

It's rare that a donor will call you back immediately after your first attempt. Remember, they're busy (as are you). They have a company to run, a family to take care of, social obligations to fulfill, and a life to live. Unfortunately, you and your nonprofit are seldom at the top of their list of priorities. But the more persistent you are in your follow up, the greater your chances of getting a call back.

What's the best way to build rapport with someone when I haven't even spoken to the person yet?

It's true that donors are more apt to call you back if they like you or feel a sense of connection with you. So how do you develop that before even speaking to them? One way is to leave a message about something important to the donor.

For example, I once was trying to reach a man who I knew was an avid fly fisherman. I had left several messages with no reply. About a month later I learned that a fly-fishing convention was coming to town. So I called him again and left a message stating, "Hi Jack. I called to let you know that there's a fly fishing convention coming to town. I have the details about it. Call me back and I'll fill you in."

A few hours later, he called me back. Of course, I gave him the details of the convention, and then I made my "ask" for my organization. He wrote me a check that day.

Another way is to find someone who knows the person you're trying to reach. Then when you leave a message, you can say, "Hi Monica. Lisa Peterson at the University said I should call you. She mentioned that your organization is trying to [state something you've learned they are trying to do that ties to what your organization does]. My organization has similar interests. I'd love to discuss this more with you."

Find whatever triggers you can that will create desire and interest in the other person. That's what prompts a return call.

What's a good approach for timing follow up phone calls?

No one wants to appear like a stalker, calling a donor every day. My advice is to call three times within a two-week period. If there's no reply, then let it go for a week or two. Psychologically, this makes people wonder, "Why isn't she calling me anymore?"

After that week or two break, call again, and this time relate the message to something the person has an interest in, such as, "Hi. I haven't heard from you. Did you know that X is happening in the community? You need to be a part of that. Give me a call and I can fill you in."

Is it always a phone call? Can't I just send an email?

You can certainly send an email. The problem is that most busy executives get literally hundreds of emails each day, so there's a high chance yours will get lost. Of course, if you've tried calling for months and can't get a reply, then by all means send an email.

When you do use email, try to attach an article of interest so the person sees value in opening your message. Then, you can call and say, "Hi. I thought you might like to know that [insert whatever the pertinent article topic is you're going to send]. I'm going to email you an article about it. Take a look and give me a call."

If you still don't get a reply, you can call and leave a message stating, "I sent you a great article about X. I hope you've had a chance to read it. I have some ideas about it too. Give me a call."

Do whatever you can to pique their interest. What do you know about your donor that you can use to build interest and rapport?

Chapter 8
What to Say to Donors...and What Not to Say

You received a return call from your donor (or you got through directly), you've made an appointment with them, and you've shown up (on time) at the person's office or a neutral meeting spot, like a café. Now that you have the person sitting in front of you and their full attention, what do you say? How do you get the donor to contribute?

This is your time to shine. What you say (and don't say), as well as how you guide the conversation, will determine whether you leave empty handed or with a commitment for a contribution.

What are some killer opening questions to ask?

A few of my favorite questions to ask at the beginning of a conversation with donors include:
- "Mr. Smith, when I say [insert the name of your organization], what one word comes to mind?"
- "Ms. Jones, what positive things do you see [insert the name of your organization] doing in the community?"
- "Mr. Peters, what one thing would you like to see [insert the name of your organization] do for our community?"

Questions like this are designed to get the donor's opinion and feedback, and to have them feel like they are in control of the conversation (which they really aren't—we'll get into that in a moment).

What are some questions to never ask a donor?

A common concept in coaching is that there are no dumb questions. When talking with donors, however, there are some very dumb questions that should never come out of your mouth. They include:

- "Have you ever heard of [insert the name of your organization]?" (If they say "no," then why should they support you?)
- "Tell me about your company." (You're approaching them for money, so you should know all about them already.)
- "What will it take to get you to support [insert the name of your organization]?" (This conjures up images of the old, stereotypical used car salesperson. Don't go there.)

Additionally, if you mispronounce the person's name, you're heading for trouble. With all the diversity in today's society, it can be difficult to say someone's name correctly. If you're meeting with someone who has a tricky name to say, practice saying it beforehand.

Do I need to know everything about my organization and how it operates when I talk to a donor?

You don't need to know the nuts and bolts of your nonprofit. Too often people get stuck and think they have to know every single thing about the organization, so they spend hours and hours researching but never talk to a donor.

To raise money for your cause, you don't need to know every minute detail. Sure, you need to know where the money is going, what kind of programs your nonprofit offers, what kind of results they get, how your organization impacts the community, and other surface level information. But you don't need to know how the program works minute by minute, who makes what decision day to day, and other nitty-gritty details.

You also need to know if the money given is tax deductible. There are some rules in fundraising and how taxes apply. You can find out through your state's standards program how that works in your area.

How do I stay in control of the conversation?

Remember this old sales saying: "He who asks the questions controls the conversation." In other words, you need to ask questions of your donors rather than simply tell them everything you know.

The best fundraisers ask questions—lots of them. If you go in to your meeting and spend all your time telling the other person how wonderful your organization is, that won't get you the results you want.

The key to getting the person to donate is to know what their passions are—to know what interests they have in the community and what they want to see happen. The only way to know those things is to ask.

And yes, it's okay to ask personal questions … as long as you phrase them correctly. For example, suppose you're raising money for an organization that supports cancer research and you've heard through the grapevine that the person you're talking with recently lost their father to cancer. Since it's not pubic knowledge, don't say, "Isn't it true that your dad died of cancer?" That's tacky and obtrusive. Rather, you could ask, "Do you know someone who has had cancer?" The person will likely reveal the personal connection.

If the person you're talking with has a personal story that's been featured in the news, it's okay to relate that to your cause. For example, if you're raising money for a cause that fights drunk driving, and the person you're talking with was featured in the news because their son died as a result of a drunk driver, you could say, "We understand that you are fighting to rid the roads of drunk drivers. That's exactly what our organization does. Can we count on your support?"

The key is to use your questions to lead the conversation and ultimately the donor to a "yes" reply. What questions are you going to ask at your next donor meeting?

Chapter 9
Go for "The Ask"

All fundraising ultimately comes down to "the ask," which is nothing more than you asking the donor for what you want. If you never ask, you'll never get. But you don't want to risk asking at the wrong time. You need to do your "ask" at the right moment, and in the right way.

What is the best time to do "the ask" when speaking with a donor?

Even though "the ask" is akin to "the close" in sales, you don't want to wait until the end of your conversation to bring it up. In fact, the best time to ask is at the beginning of the meeting. In other words, start at the end.

Of course, if you're doing an event where you're hosting a dinner, typically at the end of the meal someone comes up to speak and asks everyone to break out their checkbook. That's fine for that venue.

When you're talking one-on-one with a donor, especially a CEO who doesn't have a lot of time and who knows why you're meeting, you don't want to waste time. Often, the person can only spare 10 to 15 minutes with you, so you better ask right up front or you may miss your chance.

What's the best way to phrase "the ask"?

All questions to your donor, especially your "ask" question, should be open-ended. In other words, don't ask a question that prompts a "yes" or "no" reply. So rather than ask, "Will you give $10,000 this year?" ask, "How much are you giving this year?"

This approach has two benefits:
1. You're "assuming the sale" and not giving the person a chance to say "no."
2. You're not pre-selecting how much the person will give. If you ask for a dollar figure, and the person was actually thinking about giving more, he or she may think your figure is all you need so that's all they'll give. In this case, you could get less than what the person was planning. That's called leaving money on the table.

It takes practice to be direct, but donors at higher levels will respect you more when you are.

Of course, they may reply with questions for you, such as:
- "What value is the community getting from my money?"
- "What is your organization doing differently this year?"
- "How, specifically, is my money being spent?"

This is when you go into the details of what your cause does—after "the ask." You can talk about how many people your organization has helped, specific programs you're offering, success rates for your programs, etc.

What signals do you look for to get commitment from the donor?

When you're talking face-to-face with a donor, always look at the person's body language, as that often gives away more about what the person is thinking than their words.

Are they acting distracted (doodling, tapping their fingers, looking at their phone), like they'd rather not be there? Is their body "closed" to you (arms crossed)? Or are they engaged and making eye contact? Are they leaning in to talk with you? Reading body language is a skill that you need to practice. After all, someone could have their arms crossed because the room is cold. So look at the whole picture, not just one element, and read all the cues around you to determine how the meeting is really going.

Above all else, don't be afraid to be direct with your ask. Remember the old saying, "Ask and you shall receive." Who are you going to ask today?

Chapter 10
Overcome Rejection

S ometimes, the donor will tell you "no." That's okay, because a "no" doesn't always mean "no." Often, a "no" is a "maybe" or a "tell me more" in disguise. The good news is that you can turn a "no" into a "yes."

What's the best way to turn a "no" into a "yes"?

To begin, make sure you cover all the known objections you routinely hear in your main presentation. Typically, every organization has a few objections they hear over and over. Since you know you're likely to hear those objections, deal with them head-on before the donor has a chance to mention them.

Also, when someone says "no," they typically give a reason, such as, "No. This is not in our budget for this year." If they don't give a reason, ask for one by stating, "What's making you say 'no'?"

When you know the reason behind the "no" you can combat it and turn it into a "yes."

Are there any tools you can recommend to help me develop my objection countering skills?

I keep (and regularly review) a list of comebacks to objections I often hear from prospective donors. I can provide some examples, but you know your donors best. Start listening and create your catalog of comebacks to overcome objections or rejections from your donors.

Use open-ended and closed-ended questions to your advantage. Know the difference between an open-ended question and a closed-ended question. Open-ended questions could give you valuable information about the donor. Closed-ended questions gives you a simple "yes or no" answer. Which would you prefer? If you answered, "it depends on the situation" you are correct!

It's not easy this application takes practice. I recommend a daily practice of using open-ended questions. When asking for donations phrase your question in a way that the donor must answer with a feeling or their giving intentions. Your questions should start with the "W's" – who, why, what, and how. When you put the "W's" questions into practice - remember the most valuable rule of thumb - you will gain valuable information about the donor.

Here are samples of open-ended questions:

"I see you have been a donor of [Your organization name here] in the past, what does the organization mean to you?"

"Congratulations on being named one of the *Top 50 Women in Business.* What do you feel contributed to your success?"

"I see you give to [another organization name], what information can I provide you about my organization for you to give?

Here are samples of close-ended questions:

"Would you like a cup of coffee?"

"Will you give to my organization?"

If you forget and ask a closed-ended question, you can quickly recover by asking a more specific question.

"Why have you come to that conclusion?"

Why do my donors keep saying "no"?

If you constantly get a "no" from donors, you need to do some more question-asking—but this time of yourself. Evaluate your approach.

- Are you asking questions?
- Are you asking the *right* questions?
- Are you filling the donor's need?
- Are you personable?
- Would you give to you?

If you're not sure of your approach or how you come off to others, then ask a trusted colleague or friend and let them know you don't want a sugarcoated answer. Ask them to be brutal and give you the truth. The more you evaluate your skills and then make positive corrections, the better your fundraising results will be.

From controlling the conversation to giving "the ask" to combating objections to assessing yourself, questions are the key to success. What questions are you going to ask today?

Chapter 11
Stay the Course

Rejection hurts, and giving up is all too easy. When someone says "no" to you, even after you employ the key questions and tactics from Chapter 10, you have to stay the course. You have to hang in there. Remember, a "no" doesn't always mean "no."

If you immediately quit after someone says "no," that means you don't believe in what you're doing. And if you're going to quit that easily when somebody says no, then that means you're in the wrong field. You shouldn't be doing fundraising.

The general rule of fundraising is that most donors give after the seventh attempt. That means they've said "no" seven times before saying "yes." Therefore, you have to ask at least seven times before someone responds favorably. Additionally, when the donor sees that you're hanging in there and are persistent, you'll win them over.

Is there ever a point when you have to throw in the towel?

Of course, you may get to a point when a donor says, "I told you 'no' and that's it!" In this case, you may want to pull back for now, but still follow up with them next year.

Or, you could nicely say, "Apparently this is not a good time for you. When would you like me to come back to discuss this?" If they get nasty and yell out, "Never!" then that's your cue to leave. It's not worth the fight anymore. But usually, when you're nice and showing consideration for them, they'll tell you to come back next month, next quarter, or next year.

But I really believe in my nonprofit's mission. How can I get people to see what I see?

If someone keeps rejecting you and you truly believe in your heart that this is the perfect match for your donor to help the community, you could say, "Mr. Redding, I must be doing something wrong because you continue to reject me. I believe that my organization is the best, and we offer the best value to help underprivileged children in the community [or whatever your nonprofit does]. Can you help me better understand how we can best help the community [or provide value back into the community]? What would *you* like to see us do?"

When you use this approach, you're going back to them, putting the ownership on them, and allowing them to make decisions. By considering their input, you're increasing their ego. And by asking and not telling, you're showing them you have a very strong belief and commitment to your organization and to what it does for the community.

Of course, if the person still doesn't see what you see, and if the person is getting agitated by your presence, it may be time to back off—at least for now.

Ultimately, your level of commitment and perseverance is directly related to your belief in your organization. How strong is your belief?

Chapter 12
When Donors Leave

It's a fact of business and life that sometimes you'll lose a donor. Yes, it's painful. Yes, it's confusing (especially when the person has given every year for the past decade), but it does happen. But rather than whine and complain about it (or use it as an excuse to not do better), you need to find out the reason behind it. When you do, not only can you win the person back, but you can also stop a potential trend from occurring, where a stream of people suddenly stop giving.

Why, specifically, do people stop giving?

That's the question you need to ask your donor. If you are losing donors you need to find out why, and the best way to do that is to ask: "What is influencing your decision to not give this year?"

It's a simple question but it can reveal so much. The reasons you uncover can range from something your cause did or didn't do to something you personally did or didn't do to something internally within the individual or his or her organization. However, you don't know unless you ask.

Do we need to establish a Planned Giving Project?

All nonprofits need a Planned Giving Project. Let's face it, the philanthropic generation (the Baby Boomers) is getting older and soon their numbers will start to decline. That will definitely impact the number of donations you're able to get. One way to prevent that falloff is to create a Planned Giving Project. Also, when you have a Planned Giving Project in place, it can help cushion you when a regular source of income is no longer there, such as when a funding grant falls through.

Your Planned Giving Project is an entirely new campaign to promote to those donors who have been supportive over the years. Even if you're speaking with a young Boomer, bring up the idea of your Planned Giving Project. Even if they say "no," you have to start the conversation early.

Encourage your long-term donors to speak with their financial advisor about it so they can fully realize all their options.

I've asked someone why they are no longer giving and they said that they are mad at the organization. How do I handle that?

The best way to handle someone who is mad at the nonprofit is to ask straightforward questions. Find out specifically what the problem is. Is it something you can personally resolve? If so, then do it. Often, you'll find that someone is mad because of some misinformation they received.

If you find that someone is mad at the organization due to reasons you cannot control, take the time to listen to what the person says. Sometimes they just need someone to vent to. For example, one nonprofit I was helping was going through a major reorganization of programs. Many donors were upset, but it was something I could not control. The organization was making the changes based on key data it had gathered, and it was happening no matter what.

While I couldn't resolve the donors' issues with the reorganization, I could hear them out. To do so, I met with the upset donors weekly and just listened to their concerns. I educated them about the reorganization as best as I could. I assured them the new programs would be just as beneficial to the community as the previous ones. And I ultimately had to tell them that the reorganization was happening whether they wanted it to or not.

Some people did stop giving completely, but not all did. Some eventually understood and remained committed to the organization and its new direction.

Should you find yourself in a situation where donors are upset at the organization for something you cannot control, make sure you engage in positive marketing and branding of the organization. Keep people informed of how the nonprofit runs, the programs it offers, how different divisions of the organization work together (or how they don't if they're completely separate entities). For example, many people know that the Salvation Army runs retail stores and has an adult rehabilitation center, but they don't know that those two programs are separate from each other.

So the bottom line is to deal with leaving donors and upset donors head-on. Listen to what they say and offer either a solution or some education about the organization. Not everyone is going to be happy with your answer, and that's okay. As long as you're staying focused on the mission, vision, and values of your organization, you'll persevere through thick and thin. Who are you going to listen to today?

Chapter 13
Manage Your Time...Or It Will Manage You

As a fundraiser, you have lots of things to do on any given day. We all do. That's why time management is so vital to success. When you can manage your time well, you can get more done in a productive and effective way.

We're all given the same amount of time every day to get our tasks done. So why is it that some people accomplish everything on their to-do list with grace and ease, while others accomplish only a fraction of equally as demanding tasks and bemoan the fact that they "have no time"? The secret is to not just manage your time, but to also TAKE CONTROL of it.

But what if I really don't have enough time?

When you constantly tell yourself, "There's not enough time," guess what? You won't have enough time. How about telling yourself that you do have time?

I went back to school later in life. I attended full-time, worked full-time, and took care of my family as a single mom. When I completed my classes, I was on the Dean's List, and I was excelling at work. Plus, my family still liked me. So when someone says to me, "I don't have enough time," I tell them, "You're full of it. Stop whining."

You do have the time! As I always say, "Wherever you are, whatever you're doing, the time is always the same. The time is now."

If you're not getting something done, you're likely procrastinating. Fortunately, it's never too late to turn around and get things done. For example, recently my brother decided that he wanted to open a restaurant. When I asked him when he was planning on doing it, he said, "I don't know. I'm 45. When am I going to have the time to do it?"

I looked at him and said, "Today! If you want to do it, then do it!"

A few weeks later he opened his restaurant. So again, the time is now. You need to take control of your life. That's the only way to manage it.

 How can I get a better handle on my schedule?

Look at what you've been doing over the past few weeks—both professionally and personally. What are you spending your time on? You may say that you have no time, but really look at what you're doing during the day.

- Are you spending three hours each night watching TV?
- Are you wasting five hours online surfing the web or social media sites?
- Are you not planning your routes for donor visits effectively—constantly zipping back and forth across town or counties rather than clustering your visits?

Really analyze your schedule to see where your time wasting activities are, and then get **RID** of them.

Something I learned long ago was that the best way to control my time and become a better person was to shut the television off. These days I'd expand that to include shutting off social media sites (unless I'm using it to find out information about a donor). Get rid of the distractions that take you away from what you really want to do. That's the best way to get a handle on your time.

Controlling your time is a choice. What choices are you going to make today to ensure you have enough time to get it all done?

Chapter 14
The 4 Biggest Mistakes a Fundraiser Makes

We all make mistakes. There's no shame in that. But are you learning from your mistakes? Are you picking yourself up and changing course so you don't make the same mistake again?

When it comes to fundraising, there are four main mistakes I see fundraisers make. Beware of them, and how to fix them, so they don't derail your efforts or your career.

Mistake #1: Getting into fundraising for the wrong reasons.

If you don't love what you do, if you don't have a passion for the organization you're working for, your success is going to be a long and hard road. Unfortunately, I've seen some people get into fundraising because they view it as just another sales job.

I can sell anything, they think. You may be a great salesperson, but if you don't truly believe in the organization's mission, you'll have a hard time getting people to give to your cause. Plain and simple.

Mistake #2: Not realizing that you're attitude controls your success in fundraising.

Are you genuinely happy to be doing what you do? Do you believe in yourself and your organization? Do you view the world in a positive or negative light? Your answers to these types of questions will determine your attitude, and your attitude determines your success.

The people you speak to every day, whether via phone or in person, can pick up on your true attitude, regardless of the actual words you use. You know this is true, because you do it to others too. For example, you've likely gone into a retail store to purchase something and have had to interact with salespeople who'd rather not be there that day. Even if the salesperson answers all your questions and rings up your transaction quickly, you can sense if the person cares or is just there to collect a paycheck.

Your donors can sense the same thing in you! So make sure your attitude is one that donors will want to interact with.

Mistake #3: Continually blaming other people or events for your failures.

It's very easy (and very tempting) to blame others for our failures. But at the end of the day, the only thing that really determines your success is you.

Blaming others is nothing more than excuse making. How many times have you heard someone say (or have you said), "I didn't bring in any money today because...

- ...I didn't have a new brochure to give out."
- ...my contact didn't give me a proper referral."
- ...the economy is really bad."

- ...I heard that people aren't giving what they used to."

The list of excuses and blaming is endless.

Here's the truth: If you're in the right job and have the right attitude, there's no need to blame anyone or anything else. You can fundraise without a brochure, without a proper referral, and without a booming economy. Fundraisers still bring in the big money; you just have to approach it wisely.

Mistake #4: Trying to sell the organization rather than getting people to give to the organization.

Always remember that you're raising money, not selling cars or some other tangible item. So you can't "sell" the organization. Your role is to show donors the value your organization brings to the community. People give money when they believe in your cause. You gain that belief by asking questions, uncovering their passions, and showing how the organization aligns with the person's interests. Attitude and passion are what generate funds, not fancy salesmanship.

$$\text{Attitude} + \text{Passion} = \text{Results}$$
$$(A+P=R)$$

No matter what mistakes you've made in the past, you can overcome them and change your approach. Which of these mistakes have you made in the past? How are you going to change your approach so you don't make them again?

Chapter 15
Make Yourself Stand Out

Chances are the donors you're approaching are also being approached by fundraisers from other nonprofits. After all, the other organizations have the same database you do. Whether you're a small community organization or a national one, how do you set yourself apart?

Since any organization only has a certain percentage of their funds earmarked for philanthropic causes, you need to stand out in their eyes. In fact, when they think about which nonprofit to support, you want them to think of you and your organization first. It's a tall order, indeed, but it can be done!

How do I stand out from all the other people and nonprofits doing fundraising?

In order to stand out, you need to focus on three key things: Credibility, Consistency, and Follow Up.

- When you're **credible**, people believe that you'll do what you say you'll do. They see you as someone of your word and are eager to do business with you. You develop credibility by being honest, trustworthy, and transparent—you don't hide details and you "tell it like it is" in a tactful way.

- To be **consistent** means that the image you put out is the real you 100% of the time. You're not putting out the image of a business professional and then dancing on the tables at the bars on the weekends. Of course, a lack of consistency doesn't have to be that extreme. Someone once paid me a great compliment. They said, "You make every person you meet feel like the greatest person in the world and your best friend." Now realize that I'm not a "hugger" or overly friendly. But when I run into people on the street, I stop and chat with them. I ask how they are (without asking for a contribution). In other words, I consistently work on the relationship even when I'm not formally meeting with them. By being consistent like this, I develop strong relationships with donors, making it easier to ask them for the dollars later on. They know that I care about them and not just their money.

- We've talked about **follow up** in chapter seven, but it's worth mentioning again. You can't just talk with your donors when you're asking for their donation. You want to make sure you're following up with them and "touching" them throughout the year. For example, if they're getting honored for something, try to attend the ceremony. If you learned that they just had a baby, send a congratulations card. If you saw them written up in the newspaper (for something positive), write a note telling them how great it was to read about their project or initiative or whatever the article was about. Follow up shows that you're aware of what they're doing and taking an interest in them.

How do I create a personal brand for myself?

The best fundraisers not only stand out, but they also have a personal brand. Just as corporations and nonprofits each have a brand, people have brands too. It's what they're known for and how they present themselves to the community.

For example, when my donors think of me, they immediately think of someone who is prepared, who has character, and who has a passion for life. That's part of my brand—what I'm known for. When someone meets with me, they know that I've done my research. I already know whether the person I'm meeting has a passion for the organization I'm representing. Whether through actual research or good questioning during casual meetings and networking functions, I am prepared and ready to ask for the funding.

The key to creating a personal brand is to figure out how you can present yourself better than other fundraisers. Often, this means stepping up your game and becoming a better communicator. It's about being excited about what you're doing. It's about asking good questions to learn about the person you're meeting.

So what can you do that's different or exceptional to set yourself apart? What can you become known for in your niche? Being like everyone else is the not the key to success; rather, it's about setting yourself apart and being known for something great.

I know it's difficult to gather the courage to break from the pack. For many years of my life, I always felt like a square peg trying to fit into a round hole. I never felt like I fit, although I tried very hard to, and I struggled with that. It was only when I gave myself permission to embrace who I was—to be confident being the one doing things differently—that I started seeing what was possible.

You want to be that one person who stands out—who has a compelling brand. When you can do that, donors will welcome you with open arms.

What's the guru's secret to really standing out?

I've mentioned this before, but my favorite way to stand out is to send people handwritten notes. Let me say it again: handwritten notes…handwritten notes…handwritten notes. Did I mention handwritten notes? But this is only the cherry on top. Before sending the note I become the NPO guru by owning my brand, by having credibility to fundraise with ethics, and by bringing value to the donors. In other words, I live by the advice I outline in this book, and I personally do everything I recommend that you do.

When it comes time to send the handwritten notes, I have something personalized and meaningful to write in each, and I actually write them myself. This will take time, but it's worth every minute. I know there are services out there that will send cards on your behalf and they make the font appear like handwriting. I'm not comfortable with that because you never know what the end product looks like. Plus, even though the font resembles handwriting, it's not my handwriting. People receiving the card still know it's a computer font. That's why I prefer the good, old-fashioned handwritten note.

You can buy blank thank you cards at any discount store or card shop. Or you can opt for custom cards that have your name printed on them. You can even use stationery in lieu of a card. It's up to you. The key is actually writing out the note yourself, in longhand. That's what really makes you stand out.

Apparently, I'm not the only successful fundraiser that employs this technique. One of my past neighbors ran one of the biggest foundations in the country. Every morning I would see him on his back porch reading the newspaper. I'd often say "hi" and on occasion even ask if he'd like to join me for coffee or a morning run (since we were both up so early), and he always replied "no." He said that he needed to spend this early morning time reading the paper.

Eventually, I asked him why he was so committed to reading the paper each day. He said, "I read the obituaries. I read the announcements to see who had a baby, who got married, who is being honored, and even who is ill. Every single one of those people gets a handwritten card from me. I've been doing this every day for many years, and this is why my foundation has one of the biggest giving dollars in the country—because I touch them every day."

I admit, I don't go to the extreme he does, but I do believe in the power of handwritten notes and attribute the practice of sending them to my success. So take some time to look through your donor contacts today. Are they all seeing you as someone credible, consistent, and dedicated to follow up? Are they receiving handwritten notes from you? Who are you going to send a card to today? How are you going to truly stand out from the crowd?

Chapter 16
Creating Donor Loyalty

We'd all love to have a loyal following of donors who give to us every year. The question is how do you develop that following?

Quite simply, you earn it!

Loyalty comes when donors know, like, and respect you. But that doesn't happen overnight. It takes time and consistency to earn donor loyalty. Once you earn it, though, treat it like gold.

Okay, so how do I *earn* loyalty?

The more you show donors the value your organization brings to the community, the more loyal they'll be to you. This means you're out talking with them about your nonprofit throughout the year, not just at the time of giving. You're involved with them and their business. You know what's going on, and you acknowledge them regularly.

Additionally, you need to show that you and your organization are loyal to them! In other words, loyalty is a two-way street. For example, if your donor runs a printing company, are you using their services for your printing needs (assuming they give

you a good price)? If they can't give you the best pricing, are
you using a printer in your community, thus keeping the money
local? Or are you giving your business to an out-of-town printer
who doesn't even have a presence in your community? How
can you ask the printers in your community for money yet hire a
printer from another geographic location? That's not loyalty.

Your nonprofit needs to do business with the companies in your
community. It's about giving fair value back and forth. That's
how you gain loyalty from your donors so they keep giving to
your organization.

So is earning loyalty really about being friendly?

I often say that fundraising is really friend-raising. It's about
establishing good relationships with donors, because that's what
builds loyalty. In fact, the friendlier you are, the more funds
you'll raise.

So treat everyone as a friend. Call upon your friends when you
need help reaching someone. In return, let them know they can
call upon you when they need assistance with something … and
then give your assistance however you can. If you have a
friendly relationship with your donors, it'll build loyalty and
attract more friendly relationships to you.

Realize, too, that this friendly feeling needs to permeate every
aspect of your nonprofit. That means you have to work to instill
a friendly atmosphere in the workplace. When you have a
friendly workplace, your donors can see it and sense it. Like-
wise, if the organization is filled with conflict, donors can see
and sense that as well. If there's friction in your organization,
bring in a coach to help facilitate resolving the issue.

Always make sure your organization is filled with friendly,
helpful people who are dedicated to the nonprofit's mission.

And remember, the way you behave and the attitude you exude is exactly how others will respond to you.

Fortunately, creating a friendly environment for yourself and for other people around you doesn't cost a lot ... but it does pay off handsomely. How can you expand your circle of loyal friends?

Chapter 17
Finding New Donors

Having a large pool of existing donors you can call upon year after year is great. But at some point you're going to need to attract new donors to your nonprofit. In fact, to keep your organization healthy and strong, you'll need a large pipeline of prospective people you can call upon for funding.

The best way to attract new donors is to go out and look for them. And the best place to look is at local and national networking events. Of course, formal networking is just one tool to expand your reach. You've probably learned or tried many other options, such as getting referrals from board members and current donors, or maybe even doing a public speaking event. Those are great too. Networking, though, is the easiest way to get in front of lots of people so you can spread your message and meet new potential donors.

But I'm a nonprofit. Do I really have to network?

Many people in fundraising mistakenly believe that all those networking events they hear about aren't suited for them. They think those events are only beneficial to people in the corporate world looking for sales leads, new vendors, or alliance partners. Nothing could be further from the truth!

At the national level, you're often invited to different networking events in different communities. Attend those functions! All nonprofit organizations need to be networking in the business environment because those companies are the ones that are going to give you money.

When you attend the various networking events, be friendly, outgoing, and inquisitive. Let others know what you do and find out what they do. After telling others about the nonprofit you work for, some good questions to ask your new contact are:

- What do you do for a living?
- Tell me about your company or what you do in the community.
- What is your organization's mission or vision?
- What kinds of things in the community are important to you or your organization?

Really get to know the person and the organization they work for. That's the whole point of networking.

But make sure you don't spend all your time with one person. In fact, here's my advice for making the most of the networking event. When you go to these networking events, put 20 of your business cards in your left pocket. By the time you leave the event, you want your left pocket empty and to have 20 new business cards from new people you've met in your right pocket.

Immediately following the event, send each person you met a handwritten note. It can be short and sweet, such as, "It was great meeting you. I learned a lot about your business. I'd love to learn more. Let's have coffee. Tell me when you're available and we'll set it up."

How much networking do I really have to do?

Most successful fundraisers spend approximately 60 to 70 percent of their time networking, doing research, and meeting with potential and current donors. Therefore, I suggest you create a weekly plan that allocates a certain number of hours to key activities.

For example, you may decide to devote 12 hours to networking, 12 hours to meeting with prospective and current donors, and 6 hours to research. The remaining 10 hours of your week (assuming a 40-hour workweek) are for "other" office duties you must attend to.

Think of networking like a game. You want multiple balls in the air. Then, when it comes time to raise money, you catch one ball at a time. The more balls you have in the air, the easier it is to reach your goals because you're not scrambling to find the people you need. You've already made the connections through your networking activities; now it's simply time to win the game.

Should I get testimonials from loyal donors to attract new ones?

Testimonials are a great way to get new donors excited about working with you. I have to admit that when I first started in fundraising, I was hesitant to ask for testimonials because I didn't fully understand how powerful they could be. Today, I couldn't imagine being successful without them.

When fundraisers first hear about the idea asking loyal donors for a personal testimonial, they often say, "Why do I need one? I work for an organization that has tons of testimonials. What would some personal testimonials do for me?"

Testimonials from loyal donors build your credibility. When you meet with prospective donors, you need to build credibility and rapport. Sharing some glowing testimonials from others (even people they may know) helps you do that.

For most people, our biggest mistake is not having the courage to talk about ourselves or promote ourselves. It's easy to see why. As children, we're often taught not to brag. But promoting yourself is not bragging. It's simply showing others how you can help them. And it's perfectly okay to do that. In fact, people want that!

If tooting your own horn is difficult for you, testimonials make it easier. With a testimonial from others, you're not saying how wonderful you are; someone else is (and that gives the words more credibility too). So definitely get some testimonials; they'll make your fundraising efforts so much easier.

What's the best way to ask for a testimonial?

Before you ask for a testimonial, you have to earn it. You can't ask someone to write one for you if you're in the beginning stages of your working relationship. It's almost like a report card, so you have to have a track record with the individual and organization.

If you have that history with the person established, the next time you meet with him or her, say, "Ms. Peterson, I'm so glad you're happy with the work my organization does and our relationship over the years. I'd be thrilled if you would write a short testimonial about me and how we've worked together so that I can share it with others."

Most times the person is happy to take on the request. Sometimes they'll even ask you to write what you'd like it to say and then they'll review, make any needed changes, sign their name to it and put it on their letterhead. When this happens, gladly oblige. Focus the testimonial on what you want to highlight, whether it be your leadership skills, fundraising ability, work with key groups of people, etc.

Will the nonprofit I work for have a problem with me asking for testimonials?

Most nonprofit employers don't have a problem with their fundraisers getting testimonials because it's something you're adding to your toolbox to secure new donors. Of course, if you suspect your nonprofit may not approve, ask first. Let them know you'd be showing the testimonials to new people you meet to build your credibility.

When you have a potential new donor, a testimonial is one of the best documents you can provide to assure them there's no risk in working with you or supporting your organization. You're showing that you're a reputable professional who is respected in the community. And what prospective donor wouldn't want to work with someone like that?

Chapter 18
Assess Yourself

No matter how successful you are at fundraising, you need to regularly assess your attitude, your skills, and your level of happiness in your chosen profession. Why? Because if you could make a few simple changes and be better at what you do, wouldn't you want to know what those few simple changes are? Self-assessment is what makes that possible.

How do I assess my attitude?

Great fundraisers are there to help, so that has to be the attitude you embrace—that you're helping the community, helping the organization, and helping the members. If your attitude is only that you're fundraising to raise dollars, then that's not going to work.

What's your attitude right now? If you're unsure whether "help-ing" is naturally within your nature (it's not for many people, so don't feel bad), I suggest you take a formal self-assessment, such as the DiSC® Type Indicator, to help you determine if fundraising is the right career for you.

Aside from that, to get an accurate picture of the attitude you're portraying, ask your colleagues, friends, and family. Do they see you as being truly helpful, or just someone else asking for money?

Also ask yourself how you think others perceive you. Do you think you should work on your attitude? (Hint: There is always room for improvement.) So what's your game plan to work on your attitude? What are your goals for this aspect of your self-development?

Look at other successful fundraisers in your organization (if it's large enough) or in your community. What do you admire about them? What attributes of theirs can you develop in yourself?

Consider joining the AFP (Association for Fundraising Professionals). This group will give you some great insight into whether fundraising is the right fit for you. They also offer many programs on personal development throughout the year.

When it comes to personal development and attitude enhancing, I suggest several key activities. They are:

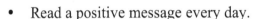

- Read a positive message every day.
- Do positive affirmations every morning when you wake up.
- Spend at least fifteen minutes a day with your affirmations and reading positive material.
- Surround yourself with positive and motivational images. My motivational picture, my "why," is to live on the beach. So I have a beautiful beach picture complete with palm trees on my phone, on my wall in my office, and as my screensaver on my computer. That's what I desire to go to, so it's visualization.
- Read fundraising books and magazines. There are plenty online.
- Read personal development books. See my recommended reading list at the end of this book.

- Read books about creativity.
- Attend at least four programs or seminars a year. The topics can range from self-help to business to personal interest. The point is to help make you a well-rounded person.
- Listen to books on CD while in your car. Again, the topics can be anything that interests you and stretches your mind.

The more you feed your mind positive and engaging materials, the better your attitude will be.

How do I assess my fundraising skills?

There's no one right way to do fundraising. It's really about knowing your personal style and what works best for you. However, having said that, there are some specific skills you should evaluate to ensure that you're incorporating them into your style.

- Are you quick on your feet when you're meeting with a donor? You never know what direction the conversation is going to go, so you always need to be prepared for the "what ifs." This includes being prepared for objections, knowing how to handle donors who are upset, and any other what-if scenario that could happen.

- Are your speaking skills finely honed? Since you're talking almost all day to donors, you want to have great speaking skills. If you mumble, use slang, say "um" every other word, or sound monotone, few people will want to spend much time with you. Therefore, to assess your speaking skills, record yourself reading a book aloud. Also record yourself during a presentation with a loyal donor (ask if they mind first). Most smart phones have a recording app. If yours does not, you can purchase a low-cost small digital recorder. After you've recorded yourself, listen to the recordings. Do you like what you hear? Would you want to listen to you? Take a public speaking seminar or join Toastmasters if you feel you need improvement.

- Are you attending regular skills training? Ideally, you should be spending 30 minutes a week in training with your colleagues or with other individuals in your community. By doing this weekly, you'll be able to keep on top of trends and be at the top of your game.

How do I assess my level of happiness?

Confucius said, "Choose a job you love, and you will never have to work a day in your life." Do you love fundraising? Do you have a passion for the organization you work for? Do you love meeting people? If you've answered "no" to any of these questions, you may need to re-evaluate whether fundraising is for you.

Today, nonprofits are much smarter. They know the organization has to run like a for-profit business and have the right people doing the right job in order for the organization to be successful. If you're not happy, you're not only hurting yourself; you're also hurting your organization.

That's why you need to honestly answer the questions: "Do I love what I do? Do I have a passion for this organization? Am I helping or hurting this organization?"

It takes a lot of pride to acknowledge any unhappiness due to being in the wrong line of work. Fortunately, if you've been a loyal employee, chances are the organization will find another position for you. Ultimately, if you hate your job and are unhappy, you owe it to yourself and your organization to speak up and change course.

Remember, fundraising isn't like a team sport. You're not competing with anyone. You're only competing with yourself. That's why you need to be your personal best. So if your fundraising dollars are low, you need to do an internal evaluation of "Am I happy?" and "Am I in the right job?"

There's no shame in admitting you're in the wrong job. Fundraising isn't a job for everyone. It takes a certain kind of person to excel. If you're that person, then great. If not, then find what you love.

Realize, too, that this does not mean you'll never have a bad day where you question why you're doing what you do. You will have those days. We all do. But every day shouldn't be a bad day.

If you love what you do, it'll be easy for you to put your whole heart into it.

Winston Churchill once said, "You make a living by what you get. You make a life by what you give." I hope this book has given you the jumpstart you need to put your heart into fundraising so you can make the most of this wonderful profession.

Now the power is in your hands. It's time for YOU to get in the fundraising groove. By raising money for your nonprofit, your work really can change the world.

Recommended Reading & Resources

Here is my list of recommended books and resources for you to investigate. Most of the books listed can be purchased through my website, www.conniepheiffspeaks.com.

Books

Three Feet from Gold: Turn Your Obstacles into Opportunities
~Sharon L. Lechter CPA & Greg S. Reid

438 Days to the Work You Love: Preparing for the New Normal
~Dan Miller

Crucial Conversations: Tools for Talking When the Stakes are High
~Kerry Patterson, Joseph Grenny, Ron McMillan, and Al Switzler

Crucial Confrontations: Tools for Resolving Broken Promises, Violated Expectations, and Bad Behavior
~Kerry Patterson, Joseph Grenny, Ron McMillan, and Al Switzler

The Tipping Point: How Little Things Can Make a Big Difference
~Malcolm Gladwell

Reaching the Peak Performance Zone: How to Motivate Yourself and Others to Excel
~Gerald Kushel

Beyond Fundraising: New Strategies for Nonprofit Innovation and Investment
~Kay Sprinkel Grace

The Wisdom of the Flying Pig: Guidance and Inspiration for Managers and Leaders
~Jack Hayhow

Donor Centered Fundraising: How to Hold Onto Your Donors and Raise Much More Money
~Penelope Burk

Resources

Association of Fundraising Professionals
www.afpnet.org

Guidestar
www.guidestar.org

Grant Smart
www.grantsmart.org

Fundraising for Dummies
http://www.dummies.com/how-to/content/fundraising-for-dummies-cheat-sheet.html

About the Author

Connie Pheiff, aka Queen of the 'ask,' is an accomplished speaker, coach, and author who presents on the topics of Change, Innovation, and Sustainability throughout the country. Connie's brand, Ignite your Passion, assists large and small entrepreneurial organizations in the areas of growth, change, and organizational leadership.

Connie has shared the stage with Bill Gates, Stephen Spielberg, and Donald Trump. Her greatest strength is her ability to not only introduce change, but also to share her strategies with an engaging delivery that corporations, nonprofits, and small business can absorb. Her experience in fundraising brings a fresh new dimension to her presentation.

Connie's greatest accomplishment is increasing membership and financial support for the Chamber of Commerce of the United States and increasing girl membership by 62 percent while CEO of Girl Scout Council.

Her two most requested speeches include *Fundraising on a Shoestring* and *If It Were Not for Other People ... Time to Take Charge.* She has worked with The United Way, The Chamber of Commerce of the United States, Hospitality Sales and Marketing Association, SHRM, The Salvation Army, Association of Fundraising Professionals, and UPS to name a few.

Connie's most recent keynote, *The Uninvited*, is a riveting story about her ability to overcome life's challenges in the face of adversity. She is a frequent guest on the radio show "The Talker" and a recurring columnist for *Region's Business Journal of Philadelphia.*

Connie uses humor to keep her audience laughing while presenting a speech packed-full of content and ready-to-implement ideas that can be utilized the moment you arrive back at your business.

She holds a MPA (Masters in Public Administration and Management), and a minor in Speech Communication, and Organizational Innovation. She is a Master Coach, and Certified DiSC® Instructor.

Connie is a member of the National Speakers Association (National & Philadelphia Chapter), Toastmasters International, and a member of several regional and state Chamber of Commerce organizations.

Connie has a passion to continue her work in the nonprofit sector through support of *Dress for Success, Susan B. Komen Foundation*, and *Girl Scouts of the USA.*

Looking for a Dynamic and Inspirational Speaker?

Call Connie Pheiff!

Connie is your #1 specialist for nonprofit and entrepreneurial coaching programs.

Her most requested keynote topics are:

- If It Were Not for Other People…Time to Take Charge of Your Life
- The Uninvited
- Do I make you uncomfortable?
- Fundraising on a Shoestring

Looking for a Career Coach who will help you find the work you love?

Contact Connie for more information at
570.341.2002 ~ 570.906.4395
info@conniepheiffspeaks.com

www.conniepheiffspeaks.com

Testimonials

"Connie was willing to share her expertise in her field to help us build exemplary assignments together. Her ability to communicate, collaborate, and contribute affected all members of the team in a positive way. I can honestly say she is one of a kind and I would be proud to work with her in any capacity. I am lucky to have worked with her and have had the opportunity to learn from her amazing skill set."

~Shawna Foster
The University of Phoenix

"When Connie Pheiff speaks … her audience listens and learns! Connie was a popular speaker at the Called Woman Conference 2013 and what a story she has to share. It is the best kind of story of all—one with a surprise ending that will encourage and inspire you to discover your calling, overcome obstacles, and live with passion. Connie's presentation sparkles and shines with her wit and powerful story. She is going to change your life"

~Lynne Watts, President/CEO,
The Called Woman Conference Atlanta, Georgia

"I have had the pleasure of working with Connie ... she is always early with her submissions and puts forth great effort in the team environment. Connie has some intriguing viewpoints on the public administration system that I have enjoyed reading and discussing with her. She is a dedicated, diligent, and hardworking woman of substance, with quality and effective leadership skills. I am really proud to recommend her."

~Sesan Popoola

"Connie is highly recommended for her facilitation skills and expertise in people management."

~Mary Jane Saras, VP Development,
Creative Energy Options

"Connie had to deal with quickly changing work environments and mergers. She used her skills to bring her team and our volunteers through the changes without adversely affecting the program."

~Linda Szoke, Director of Sales,
Split Rock Resort & Golf Club

"Connie has a wealth of organizational management skills and the ability to transfer her knowledge to the benefit of clients."

~Catherine Shafer, President,
cds creative, inc.

"Connie has proven to be an outstanding leader through turbulent times and considerable change."

~Joseph Angelella, Senior VP,
First Liberty Bank & Trust

"Connie has demonstrated impressive organizational skills. We raised over $100,000 in one week and brought in new members. We couldn't have done it without her help. Throughout my travels, often the first comment made is one complimenting Connie's talents and professionalism."

~Lonnie Taylor, Senior Vice President,
U.S. Chamber of Commerce

"Connie has exhibited great skill and polish in marketing to business leaders, piquing interest, and closing the sales. She is skilled in the full range of marketing, negotiation, closing, follow-up, and documentation."

~Jerry Lisman, VP, Marketing,
Mabis Healthcare, Inc.

"Connie is a leader in the not-for-profit arena. Her strengths involve extensive experience with strategic planning, organizational development, and motivation."

~Laura Novakowski, Co-Founder
Positive Power Strategies, Inc., 720 Thinking

"Connie delivered a flawless presentation of wit and wisdom with an entertaining twist. I highly recommend her presentation when you are looking to inspire all audiences."

~Mari Potis, VP of Events,
Scranton Chamber of Commerce

The Art of Asking: Get into the fundraising Groove is one of several books by Connie S. Pheiff. Subsequent books include Connie's life experiences from leading nonprofit organizations to becoming a leading inspirational speaker and coach for women entrepreneurs.

To be notified when additional books are published, please visit www.conniepheiffspeaks.com and sign up for automatic alerts.

Visit www.conniepheiffspeaks.com for more information

Made in the USA
San Bernardino, CA
08 March 2019